Let's Celebrate

Easter

A Book of Drawing Fun

Written by
Bonnie Brook

Illustrated by
Susan Klein

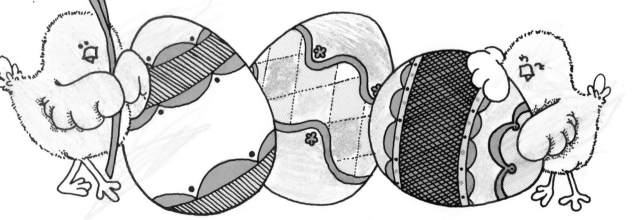

Watermill Press

Introduction

A funny bunny hops along with his basket of colorful eggs. He hides each one in a secret spot. Now the egg hunt can begin! It's the start of a special holiday—Easter is here, at last!

Imagine the sights and sounds of Easter and the very first signs of spring. You can draw your own Easter friends. It's easy! And it's fun!

Each of the drawings in this book is shown in several simple steps. Just follow each step, adding to your drawing as you go along. Soon you'll have your own Easter parade. Are you ready to begin?

Materials

You'll need paper, pencils, and an eraser to start. When your drawing looks the way you want it to, color it with crayons, colored markers, or water-color paints.

Remember, the best part of your drawing is what *you* add to it with a little imagination—so make your Easter friends any color you want. Exaggerate their features. Don't be afraid to experiment! And, most of all, have fun!

Easter Eggs

Here are a few *eggs*tra-special ideas for decorating your Easter eggs.

An Easter Basket

Brightly colored eggs and yummy candy look great in an Easter basket. What special surprise do *you* hope you'll find in your Easter basket this year?

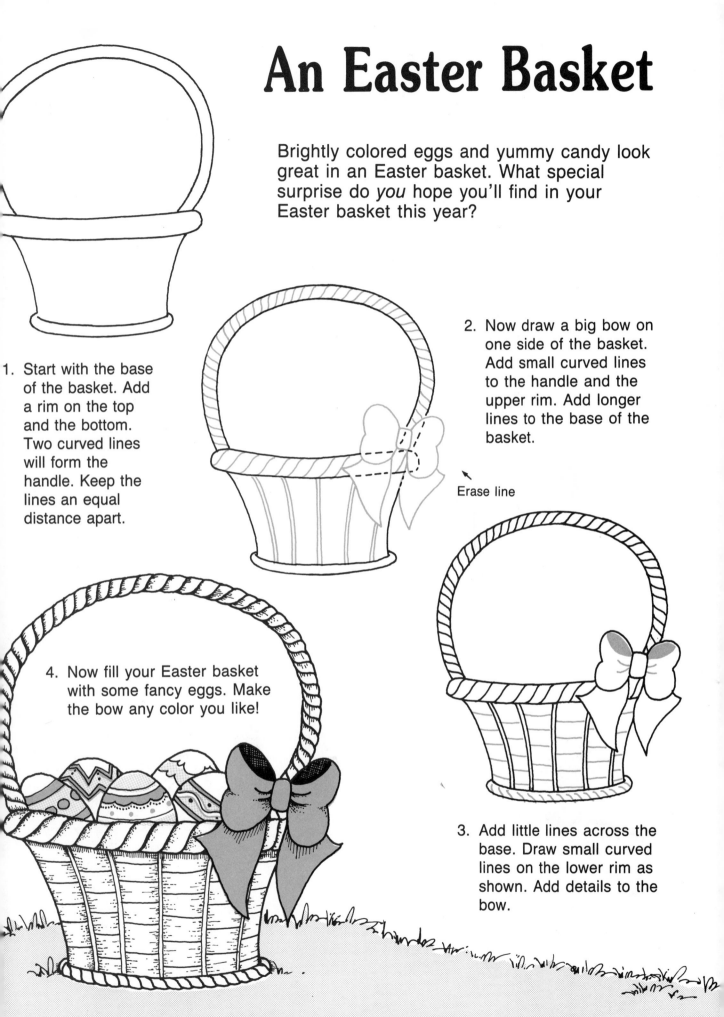

1. Start with the base of the basket. Add a rim on the top and the bottom. Two curved lines will form the handle. Keep the lines an equal distance apart.

2. Now draw a big bow on one side of the basket. Add small curved lines to the handle and the upper rim. Add longer lines to the base of the basket.

Erase line

4. Now fill your Easter basket with some fancy eggs. Make the bow any color you like!

3. Add little lines across the base. Draw small curved lines on the lower rim as shown. Add details to the bow.

Easter-Egg Decoration

In many parts of the world, people give each other decorated eggs at Easter. The decorations stand for good fortune and long life.

1. Start with an oval shape for the egg. Draw lines around the egg as shown.

2. Add zigzags at the top and bottom. Add connecting diamonds at the center.

3. Then decorate the top and bottom of the egg. Add an unbroken line of waves.

4. Add an outline above the waves as shown. Add little buds at the top and bottom of the egg.

Now fill in picture symbols of wheat and a deer on a starry night.

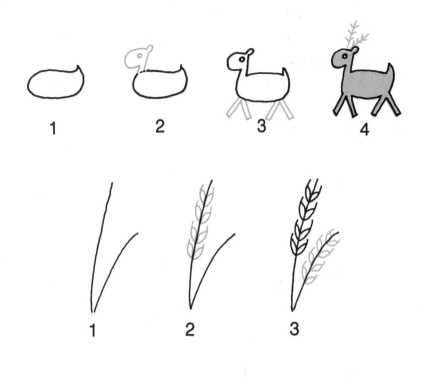

1   2   3   4

1   2   3

6. Add a crisscross pattern at the center of the egg, and color it any way you like. Then give the egg to someone you love for good fortune and long life!

Springtime in the City

Who's that bunny with the baton?
It's the Easter Bunny, of course!
He's leading a parade of his favorite friends.
Would you like to learn how to draw them?

(Turn the page and join the fun.)

The Easter Bunny

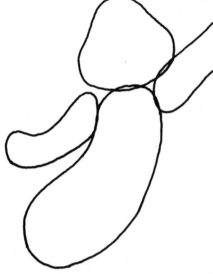

1. Start your drawing of the Easter Bunny with these simple shapes.

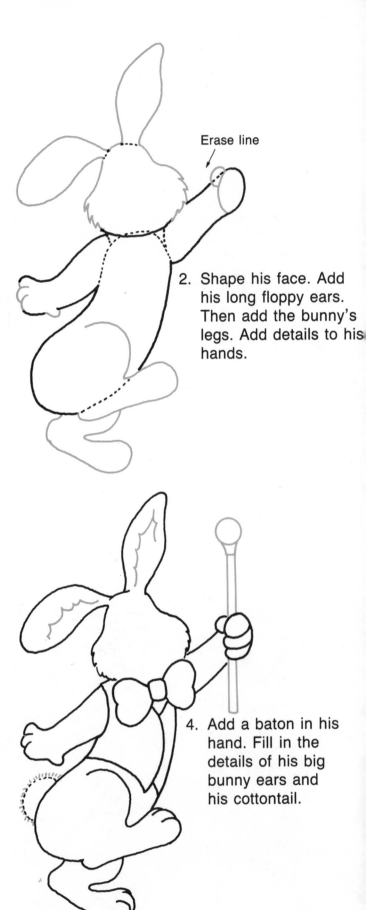

Erase line

2. Shape his face. Add his long floppy ears. Then add the bunny's legs. Add details to his hands.

Erase line

3. Add a big bow tie. Then add his vest. Add a big fluffy cottontail. Add small curved lines to his hand and feet.

4. Add a baton in his hand. Fill in the details of his big bunny ears and his cottontail.

Then fill in the details of his bow tie and vest. Give him a happy face! Make the bunny's face as silly as you like—don't be afraid to be creative!

The Easter Bunny is a funny fellow who loves hiding Easter eggs. When he isn't making mischief, he's leading the big parade!

6. Now decorate your bunny any way you like. A polka dot tie and checkered vest might be nice for the Easter parade!

In Her Easter Bonnet

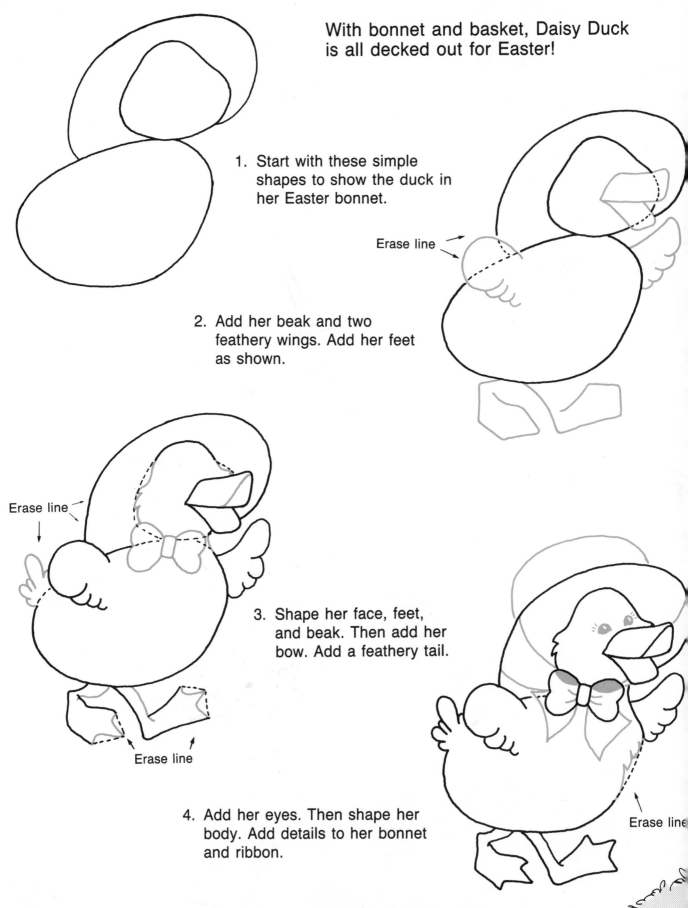

With bonnet and basket, Daisy Duck is all decked out for Easter!

1. Start with these simple shapes to show the duck in her Easter bonnet.

Erase line

2. Add her beak and two feathery wings. Add her feet as shown.

Erase line

3. Shape her face, feet, and beak. Then add her bow. Add a feathery tail.

Erase line

4. Add her eyes. Then shape her body. Add details to her bonnet and ribbon.

Erase line

Erase line

Erase line

Erase line

1   2   3

5. Now add some daisies to Daisy's bonnet.
   Add details to the brim as shown. Put a few more
   feathers on this downy duck, and she's ready for
   the Easter parade.

6. Don't forget Daisy's basket
   of flowers! They match her
   beautiful bonnet.

1

Erase line

2

3

Springtime Tulips

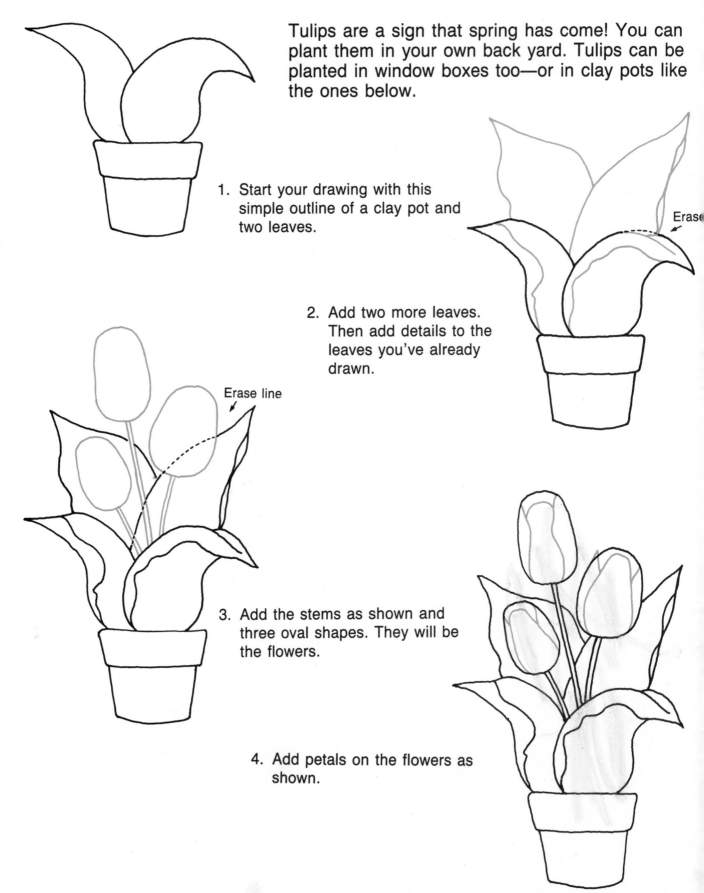

Tulips are a sign that spring has come! You can plant them in your own back yard. Tulips can be planted in window boxes too—or in clay pots like the ones below.

1. Start your drawing with this simple outline of a clay pot and two leaves.

Erase

2. Add two more leaves. Then add details to the leaves you've already drawn.

Erase line

3. Add the stems as shown and three oval shapes. They will be the flowers.

4. Add petals on the flowers as shown.

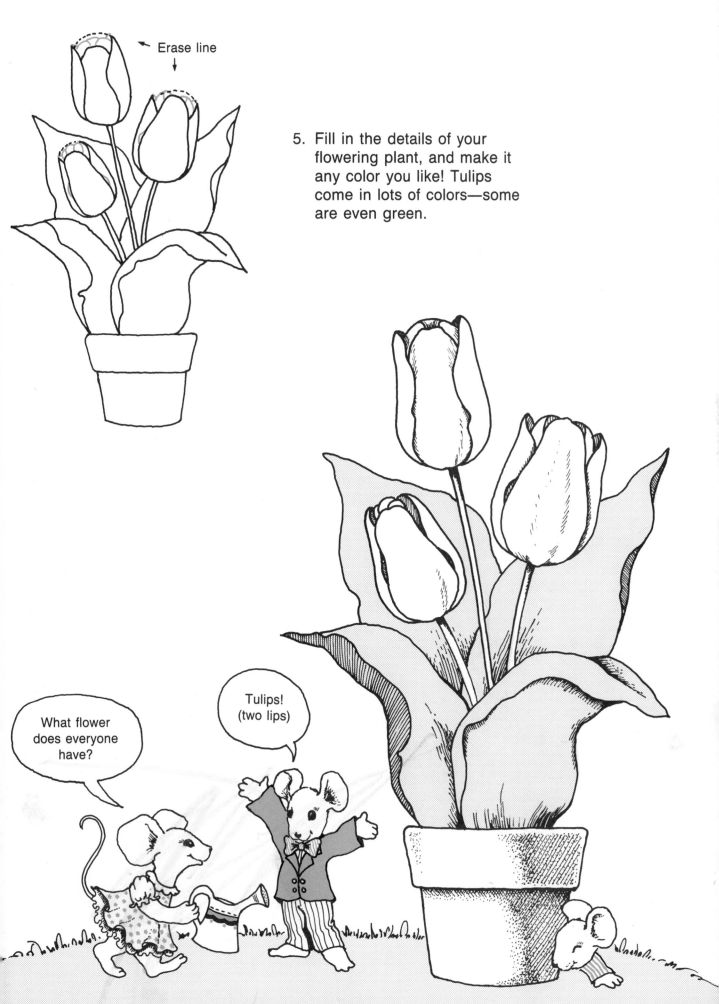

Erase line

5. Fill in the details of your flowering plant, and make it any color you like! Tulips come in lots of colors—some are even green.

What flower does everyone have?

Tulips! (two lips)

Chirp! Chirp! Chirp!

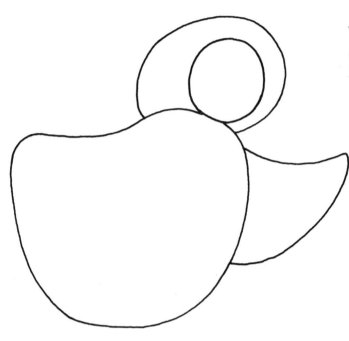

The baby chicks answer their mother's call. They seem to be saying, "Spring is here!"

1. Start with this simple outline of the mother hen in her bonnet.

2. Add her beak and the beginning of the ribbon that will tie her bonnet in place. Add another wing. Then add details to Mama's feathery tail.

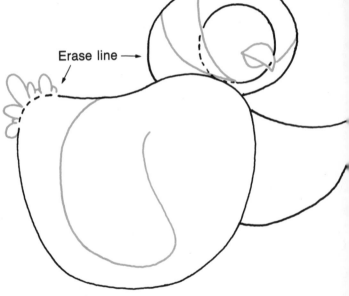

Erase line

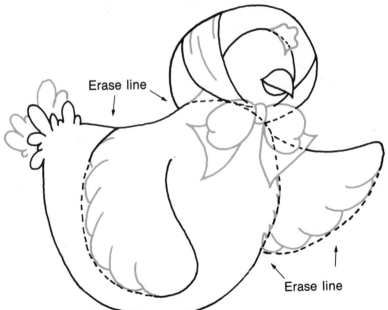

Erase line

Erase line

3. Shape the wings and the tail. Add a big bow. Add a little line for the neck. Add a crown to the top of her head. She's almost ready to go!

Now fill in more feathers and decorate the bonnet with lots of pretty flowers. Add details to the bow. Surround Mama with baby chicks. Don't forget her eyes —Mama must look after her babies!

1

2

3

The Cat's Meow!

Tom and Kitty Cat are all dressed up for the Easter parade. Would you like to draw them in their new spring outfits?

Erase line →

1. Start your drawing of Kitty Cat with these simple shapes.

2. Add the neckline of her dress and her flair skirt. Then add her ears and tail. Draw a line to separate one hind leg from the other.

← Erase line

3. Fill in the details of Kitty's dress: her lacy collar, her bow, her puffed sleeves. Add her arms and her shoes. Then give Kitty a happy face—she's going to the Easter parade!

4. Add more details to Kitty's dress and bow. Add little curved lines on her hands. Then draw a crown of flowers on her head and a flower on each of her shoes. Fill in the details of Kitty's face— don't forget her long, beautiful eyelashes!

1. To draw Tom Cat, start with this simple outline.

Erase line

2. Add his sweater, his shoes, and his ears.

Erase line

3. Add cables to his sweater. Then give him a tie! Add details to his shoes. Add his hands and a big happy face!

4. Fill in the details of his face. Draw little curved lines on his hand. Add details to the trim of his sweater. Then give him a collar with little studs. He's ready for the parade.

Color Tom and Kitty any way you like. Add a flower in Tom's hand. (See page 23.) Do you think he'll give the flower to Kitty? Draw a picture that answers this question!

Springtime in the Meadow

The bunnies are hiding the Easter eggs.
How many eggs can you find?

Daffodils, Crocuses

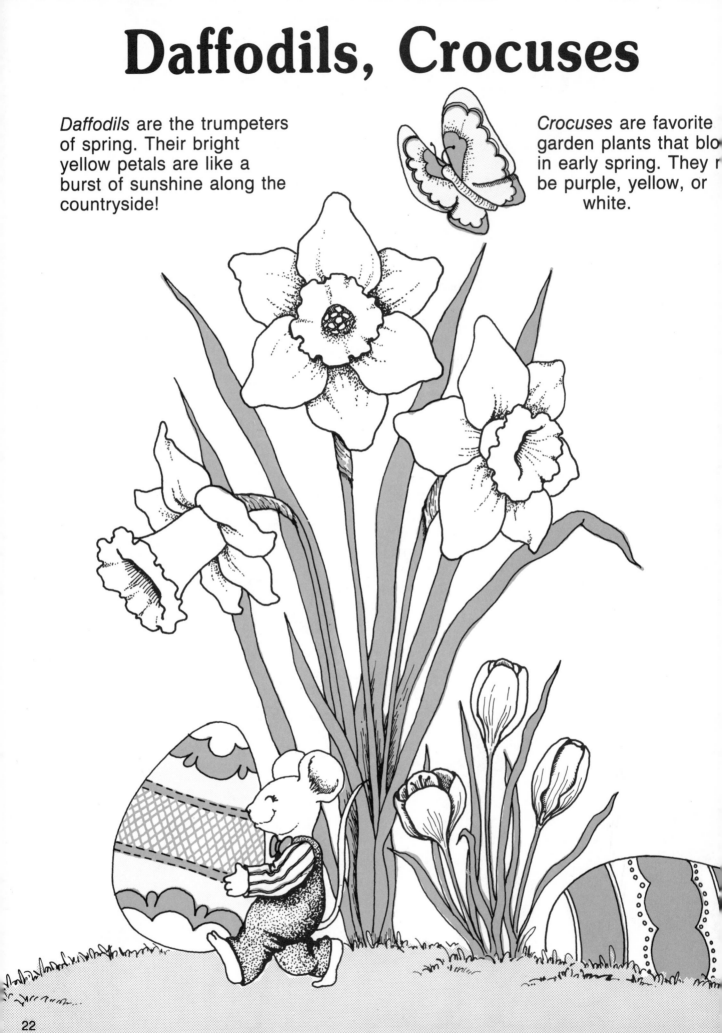

Daffodils are the trumpeters of spring. Their bright yellow petals are like a burst of sunshine along the countryside!

Crocuses are favorite garden plants that blo in early spring. They r be purple, yellow, or white.

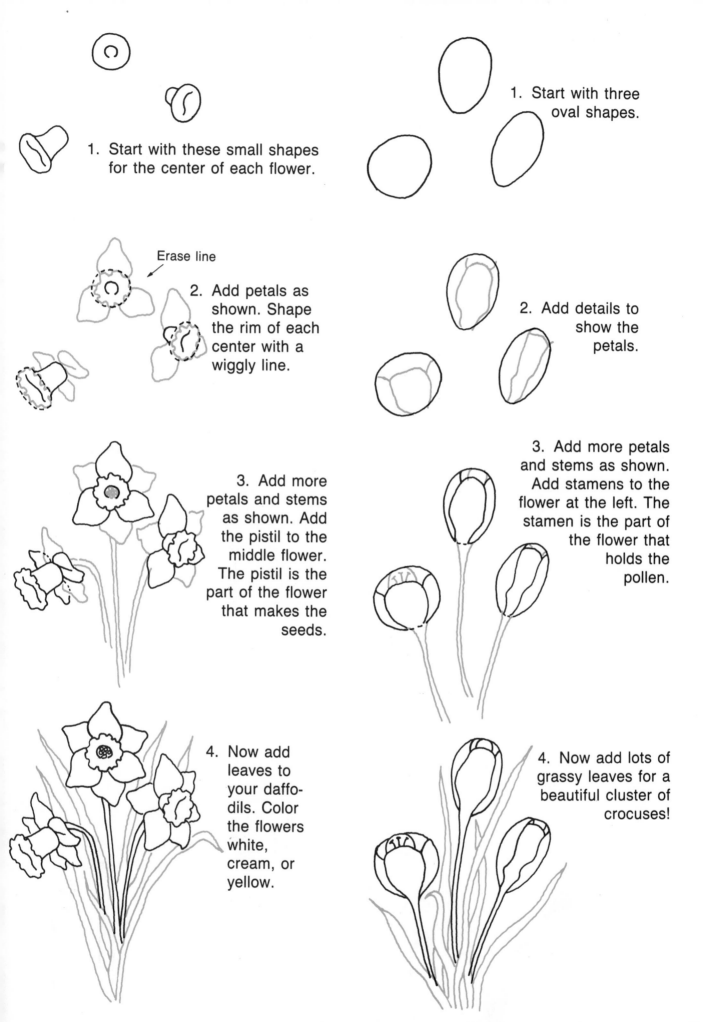

1. Start with these small shapes for the center of each flower.

1. Start with three oval shapes.

Erase line

2. Add petals as shown. Shape the rim of each center with a wiggly line.

2. Add details to show the petals.

3. Add more petals and stems as shown. Add the pistil to the middle flower. The pistil is the part of the flower that makes the seeds.

3. Add more petals and stems as shown. Add stamens to the flower at the left. The stamen is the part of the flower that holds the pollen.

4. Now add leaves to your daffodils. Color the flowers white, cream, or yellow.

4. Now add lots of grassy leaves for a beautiful cluster of crocuses!

Off We Go!

In spring the days are longer. That means more time to play! Marty Mouse enjoys a ride in a wagon pulled by his brother.

1. Start your drawing of Marty and the wagon with these simple lines and shapes.

2. Fill in the details of the arms and legs. Add two ears as shown. Add wheels to the wagon and an egg inside.

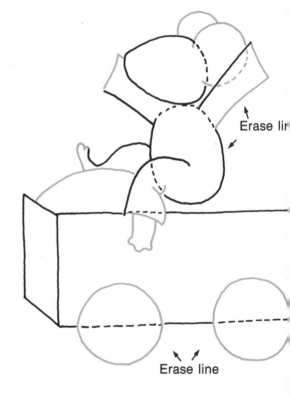

Erase line

Erase line

Erase line →

3. Add hands and a big bow tie. Give Marty a smile and shape his face and neck. Add some more eggs to the wagon.

4. Now fill in the details of his face, vest, and ear. Add a skinny tail. Add details to the wagon wheels too. Add a rope for Marty's brother to pull.

You may wish to draw the rest of this scene with Marty's brother included. Can you think of a name for Marty's brother? What's a funny name for a mouse?

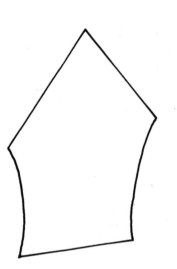

A Robin Sings

The first spring robin is a happy sign that winter is over at last. Few birds have a prettier song to welcome the season of new life.

1. Start your drawing of the birdhouse with this simple shape.

2. Add the roof and the side of the house.

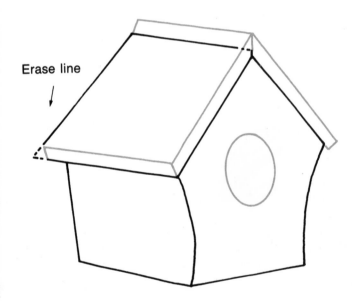

Erase line

3. Fill in details on the roof as shown. Add a circle to the front of the house.

4. Add a curved line inside the circle. Add details to the bottom of the house. Draw the pole on which the robin will perch.

Eras

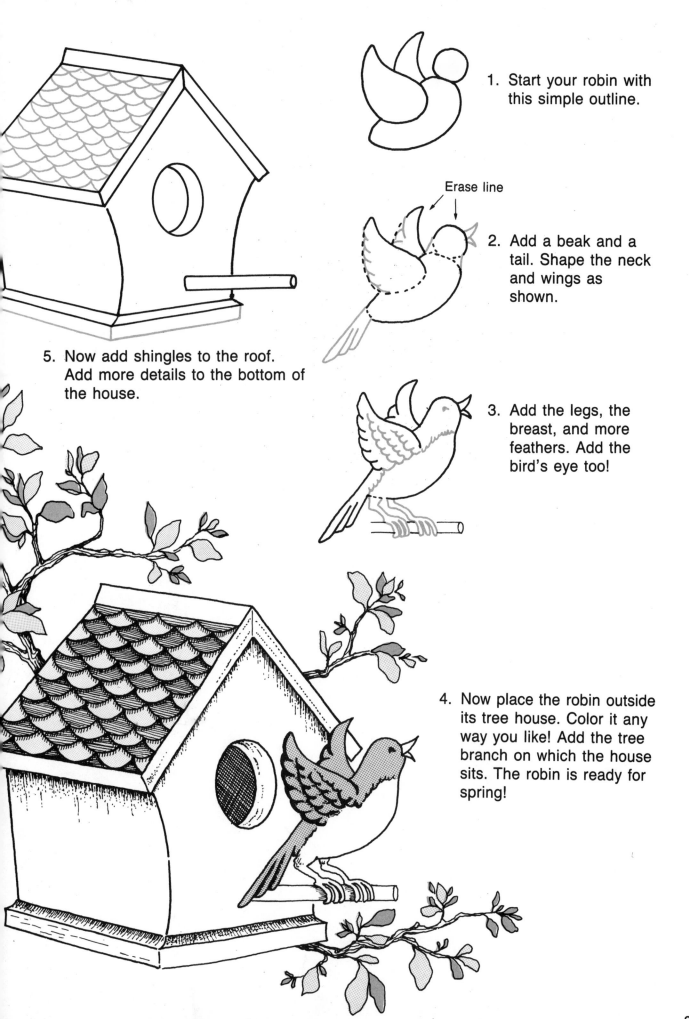

1. Start your robin with this simple outline.

Erase line

2. Add a beak and a tail. Shape the neck and wings as shown.

3. Add the legs, the breast, and more feathers. Add the bird's eye too!

4. Now place the robin outside its tree house. Color it any way you like! Add the tree branch on which the house sits. The robin is ready for spring!

5. Now add shingles to the roof. Add more details to the bottom of the house.

Butterflies Flutter By

Butterflies are the most beautiful and graceful of all the insects. They fly from flower to flower, drinking sweet liquid called *nectar*.

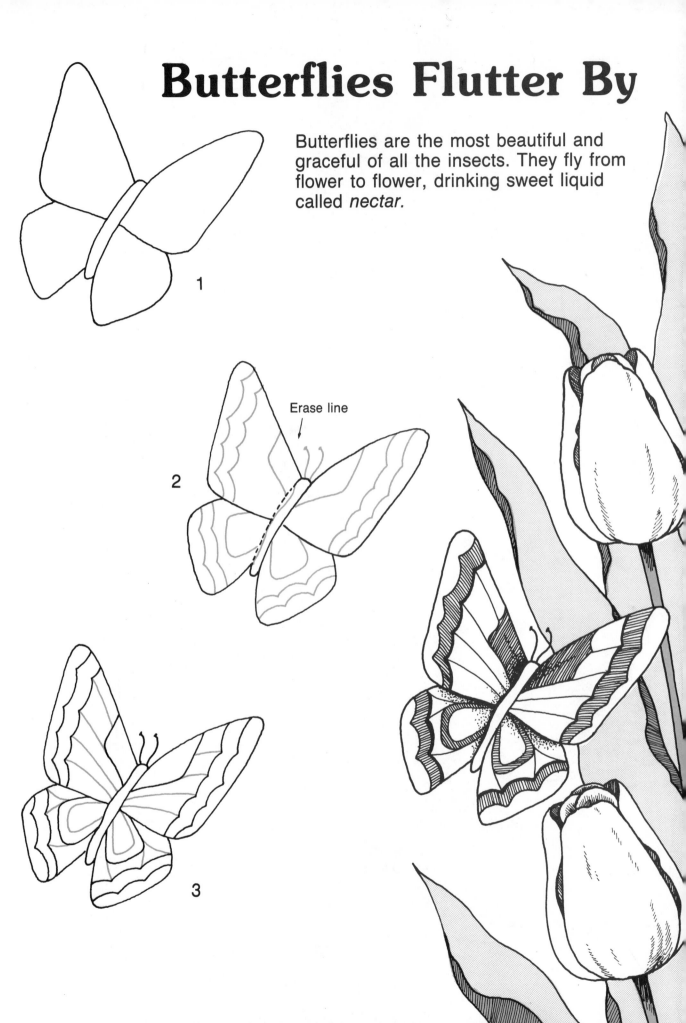

1

2

Erase line

3

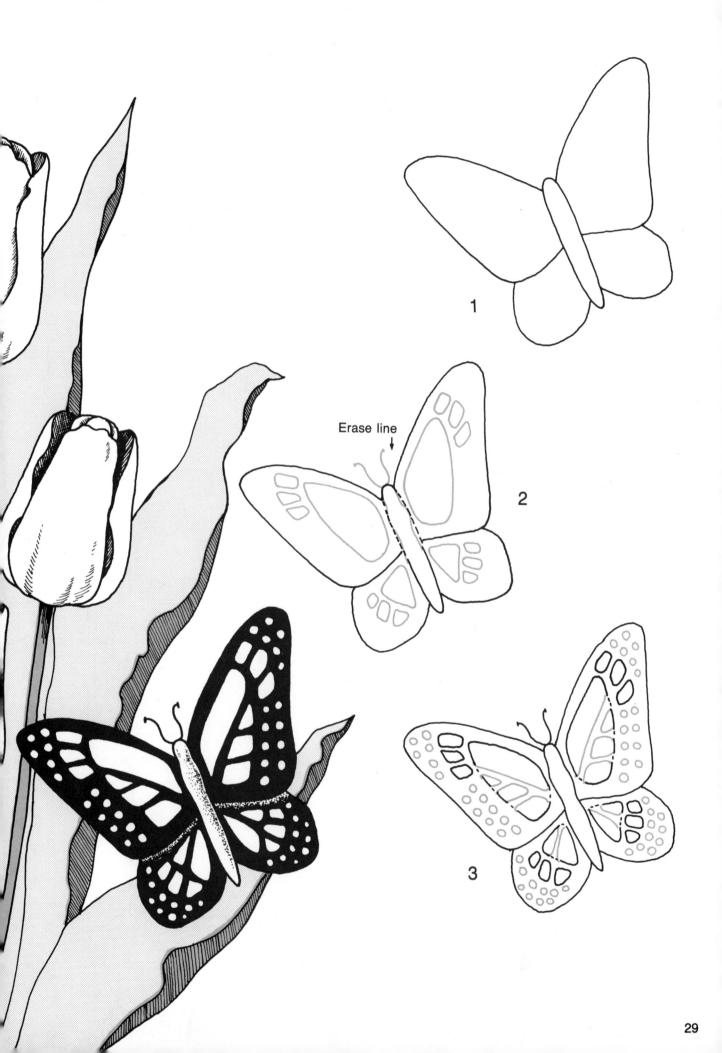

1

Erase line

2

3

Little Lamb

Spring is a time of birth. Little lambs blink their eyes. They are getting their first look at the world.

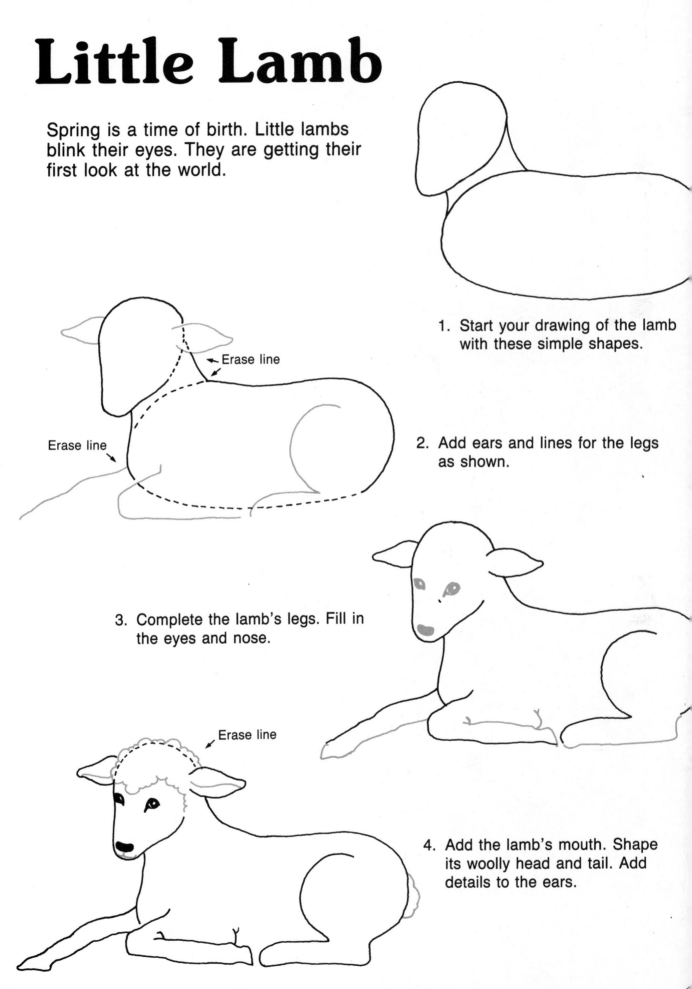

1. Start your drawing of the lamb with these simple shapes.

2. Add ears and lines for the legs as shown.

Erase line

Erase line

3. Complete the lamb's legs. Fill in the eyes and nose.

Erase line

4. Add the lamb's mouth. Shape its woolly head and tail. Add details to the ears.

5. Shape the woolly fleece as shown.

Erase line ⟶

Happy Easter!